What future for Europe after 2020?
A New European Manifesto

How to avoid the collapse of the Old Continent by resuscitating the European project

Paperback Edition, 2021
Roberto Bourbon

Introduction

The year is 1953. German officials are visiting London. It's winter. Along with colleagues from Britain, France and the US they are about to make history. A treaty is being signed. It will cancel all post-WWII debt for Germany, paving the way for a bright future of economic, social and cultural development in Europe. The treaty has a boring name: "London debt agreement". Yet, it is anything but. It will effectively allow Germany to become one of the most advanced, democratic and developed nations on Earth.

This is happening only 8 years after the end of World War II. All people signing that Treaty have lived through World War II personally. Virtually all of them have suffered from it, in a way or another. If they met less than a decade earlier, it would have been a very different meeting. Some might have been winners, some losers. Yet, there they are today, in London, as *equals*.
It is not a matter of the UK or France "forgiving" Germany for the horrors of (two) World Wars. This treaty is about letting go of the past to look at a better, more prosperous future. A future that is and *must* be built together, as equal nations.

Fast forward 57 years. It is 2010. We are in Greece and it is late spring, May. The European Commission, European Central Bank and International Monetary Fund have just launched a 110 Billion euro plan to rescue Greece from defaulting. In exchange, they are asking for Greece to implement austerity measures, drastically cutting its public expenditures. These measures will soon come into effect and will throw thousands of people in unemployment, curb Greece's growth and Welfare state for the decade to come.

This bailout fund is completely and utterly legitimate. Done in broad daylight. These are well known mechanisms that have been used by the IMF to rescue other countries in the past. The International community accepts them as a legitimate tool to rescue a country in need.
This bailout is being signed-off by a democratically elected Greek government. Surely the situation is far from ideal, but it has been caused by Greece itself and Greece only. It is Greece that has run a public deficit for too many years, spiraling its debt out of control. It is also Greece that has accepted to be part of

the European Union, it has adopted the Euro as a currency and has voluntarily agreed to adhere to its directives, regulations and budgetary rules. And it is not like the European Union is a foreign occupation army. Greece is properly represented in the European Parliament and can, theoretically, leave if it wants to at any time.

There is a substantial distinction between these two, very different, historical moments. *Solidarity*. In 1953, European nations were ready to let go of the past to allow for a better future. Surely, Great Britain or France did not benefit from cancelling Germany's debt in the short term. But they did in the long term. They allowed for Germany and Europe to grow and become the largest economic area in the world. They benefited from having strong, developed nations as neighbours with which they traded, growing themselves as a result. They benefited beyond merely economic terms. Europe knew no more wars between major countries for the next decades. It achieved all of that with just a bit of *solidarity*. Solidarity between European countries, between European people. Yet, 57 years later European people are not able to "forgive" Greece as they did with Germany. Even if, on purely moral grounds, Greece is far less of a culprit. In the worst case, you can accuse 2010s Greek people of having "lived beyond their means" (which is also a flown argument, but let's allow it for a second). In the best case, you can accuse 1950s German people of having started two World Wars and being therefore responsible for the death of millions of people.

Still, our grandparents were able to "forgive" the very same people that 10 years earlier put their families in death camps. We, today, are not able to "forgive" people that poorly managed their public accounts. Could this change with the current crisis induced by COVID-19?

This is what this short book is about. Understanding whether solidarity in Europe does not exist anymore, why it has disappeared and what we can do to reinstate it. In light of the current crisis of COVID-19, what is the future for Europe? We are going to end the book with a manifesto that challenges Europe to re-think of itself.

Solidarity

In the last 30 years Europe has lost the very principle upon which it was funded. An overwhelming majority of voters in most European countries today are not willing to concede more powers to the European Union. It is not only the Germans or the Dutch. Even in Italy or France, the EU is seen as an evil "supranational" entity that steals from a nation's sovereignty. All things considered, voters think it is better to keep things as they are.

The weird thing is that Europeans today are strongly opinionated on highly technical matters. Brexit happened while most of British voters struggled to even understand exactly what the European Union is about. Most German voters reject the ideas of Eurobond or Fiscal Union. Yet, most German voters would not be able to give a correct definition of what exactly a bond is or what Fiscal Union means.

In the USA, in contrast, most taxpayers in New York have nothing against a consistent part of their taxes going into a Federal budget. They have nothing against the US central government issuing debt. More interestingly, these mechanisms exist and work in Europe at country level as well. All major countries in Europe are based on the principle of redistributing wealth between rich people and/or rich geographical areas and poor people and/or poor areas. This is why income tax in most European countries is not linear, featuring brackets that rise with personal income. This is why some countries have special "free trade zones" and most spend a disproportionately high amount of their central budget to develop specific geographical areas. Bavarian taxpayers pay for Eastern Germany. Northern Italians for Southern Italy. Taxpayers in Paris in France maintain the welfare of most of the rest of their country. Barcelona and Madrid account for most of the budget that Spain utilizes to develop other geographical areas.

This all happens simply because it does not exist, anywhere in the world, a geographical area with similar economic, societal and cultural conditions. If Governments decided not to intervene and redistribute wealth, redistribution would happen anyway. In the form of people migrating from poor to richer areas, leaving behind unpopulated areas and resulting in overcrowded megacities.

This is the case of most African or developing countries, where central governments do not have the budget or the political will to redistribute wealth. You get to the birth of mega-cities with poor infrastructure and people living in slums. The people that own assets in the city become richer and richer, the migrants barely make a living. Poor geographical areas, slowly becoming underpopulated, are forced to become "competitive" with richer areas by becoming even poorer. The remaining workforce costs less and less, people earn less and live even worse than before. This is what happens today in Eastern Europe - where most of the former Soviet Bloc has been converted into the "factory" of Europe. It is not a secret that people in those countries today, even after 30 years from the fall of the USSR, have lower life expectancy than people in Western Europe. Lower access to healthcare, instruction and services results in lower life expectancy.

These are the two golden rules of any economical area, whether it is a country or not: either wealth is redistributed via a central authority, or you have movement of people, with resulting inequality.

To be clear, these two effects are not an "either; or" and neither of them is a bad thing per se. In most of the world, they are both happening at the same time. Citizens in the UK flock to London to find better job opportunities. At the same time, the government reinvests taxes collected in London to develop other cities and provide welfare to underdeveloped geographical areas.
Even in the USA, where a strong federal central government exists, mobility of people is very high. Americans generally have no issues in moving to a different State to find better jobs. The coexistence of both is a good system. It gets bad only when movement of people is the only element that allows for redistribution of wealth.

Redistribution of wealth via a central system happens based on one simple principle: solidarity. Solidarity between people living in a specific geographical area. Sure, there are several examples of tensions inside countries when it comes to solidarity: Catalonia's failed quest for independence, to mention just a recent one. Yet, solidarity is always a basic need for any society.

Even if a "richer area" gained effective independence from a poor one, nothing would change. Precisely because there is no geographical area with the same societal, economic and cultural conditions. You can split a country in smaller countries, and smaller countries will still have significant economic differences. There is always going to be someone richer and someone poorer. Inequality exists at country, region, city and neighbourhood level. New York is a very wealthy city by international and US standards. But it's wealth is not evenly distributed among neighbourhoods. Even if it became independent from the rest of the US, people in Manhattan would need to pay for people in the Bronx. Even if Manhattan then gained independence, there would still be richer and poorer people living in it.

Do not take this absurd and hypothetical case of New York as the only example. There are plenty of real cases in the world. After the collapse of the USSR, Yugoslavia split in different countries. Among them Slovenia, Croatia, Montenegro. Are these countries today particularly successful? Not by many measures. South Sudan recently split from Sudan. It is now one of the poorest countries in the world, in an almost constant state of civil war.

This does not even account for the loss of international relevance or power of negotiations. A small, independent, Catalonia would not have the same weight in Europe or in the world as a united Spain. But even if we assume that this is not true, the fundamental issue remains: a nation, no matter how small, will always experience economic inequality and cultural differences.

If people were not capable of accepting the principle of solidarity as part of a bigger system, they will not be able to do so even as a smaller, independent entity. For example, there are minorities in Catalonia that are against independence and /or against having Barcelona as their capital city. There will always be minorities with a different agenda than the majority. If we are to cancel the principle of solidarity, then there would be no choices but to split in smaller and smaller independent entities, looking at each other in anger and resentment.

Europe is a vastly different area, not last because of its history and culture. The principle of solidarity today in Europe was never meant to be as easily implemented as in the USA, where American citizens enjoy a common language and culture. After all, it took Europe two World Wars to finally leave its differences behind and accept some level of solidarity between countries.

Arguably, competition between European countries is what drove Europe to become "ruler of the world" up until the XX Century. It boosted achievements in sciences and economics, paving the way for the development of the world. Solidarity has substituted competition after WWII, but today is in crisis and it has apparently disappeared from Europe.

Do not blame the people

You cannot blame the voters to not want "more" of Europe. Europe as a geographical area has been stagnant for the last 20 years, lagging growth behind the USA or (obviously) Asia. Jobs are not as secure as they used to be and environmental concerns seem to be worse every year. Generally, Europe is suffering from the same problems of the rest of the developed world: stagnant wages, rising inequality, the need to reform an economic system that seems structurally outdated and unfit for the current century.

Considering that the European Union in its current form has existed for a good 30 years now, it is normal that in the eyes of voters it has not meant anything significantly positive. Life has not drastically improved under the European Union, so why should we give it more power? This is a simple mechanism. It surely is fallacious, but it is nevertheless the very principle upon which representative democracies are based. If your life has not improved under the person you voted, you are going to vote for someone else next time.

The reason behind this lack of trust in the European Union is that highly technical matters have been transformed into political tools. In the past years a clear narrative has taken place and has been de facto accepted by most European citizens. The narrative has many elements, that I try to summarize as follows:
1. There are countries that manage well their finances and countries that constantly live beyond their means.
2. The reason why certain countries live beyond their means is because, fundamentally, their citizens are lazy.
3. In case of an economic crisis, it is generally a good practice to limit public expenditure.
4. In a civil society, if you want money you have to give it back with interest.

This narrative is very simple to understand and tackles the logic of most people. After all, if you lose your job, would you buy a new fridge or TV? Isn't it true that when you go to Spain on holiday people seem generally relaxed and partying all the time? If you go to a bank, can you reasonably expect to be handed in money for free?

The problem is that said narrative simplifies very technical matters and vastly contradicts the fundamentals of macroeconomics. Put simply, the logic that applies to a household does not always apply to a country or to any economically sophisticated society.

Do not get me wrong. There is a base of truth in parts of this narrative. For example, Mediterrenean countries have higher corruption and are not efficient in tackling tax evasion. Public expenditure should indeed be limited, even if in periods of economic growth, not during a crisis.

However, fundamentally this narrative is flown. Let's try to understand why point by point:

1. True, some countries have run significant public deficits. However, this has largely been done to compensate for the lack of any wealth redistribution mechanism inside the EU. Unable to issue their own currency and presented with only small investment at central level, countries resorted to public debt to sustain their welfare and economy. The important thing to note is that this was considered an absolute best practice up to the 2010-11 sovereign debt crisis. In 2004, with the Olympics Games in Athens, Greece was considered by all European nations a success case, thanks to the generous public expenditure that fueled its growth in the last years. Spain as well was considered a booming nation with incredible growth prospects. The narrative began to change only after the sovereign debt crisis.

2. The claim that certain categories of people are lazy (or criminals, or any other adjective), is just plain false. It is no different than to say that "black people are thieves" or "jews are dishonest". These stereotypes are born from historical elements and confirmation bias: black people have been enslaved for centuries, therefore once freed they generally had limited education and accessed only the most humble jobs. To white people, every time a black person stole something it just confirmed their bias. It took decades to close the gap with white people, if it has ever been. Jews alike have historically been working with finance and money lending,

mostly because Catholics would not do so for religious reasons. We all know how the hatred towards Jewish communities degenerated in the XX century.

Obviously the narrative that today is applied to specific countries in Europe is not comparable to the ones perpetrated towards Jews or black people in the past. Yet, it is worrying that it is present and widely accepted by European citizens in 2020. Fueling apparent diversities between classes of citizens has always been a trigger for conflict. It is undeniable that in today's Europe, there is a perception of "class A" and "class B" Europeans.

3. The fact that public expenditure should be limited in time of crisis is just plain false. As counter-intuitive as it might sound to the man of the street, sustaining the economy with increased public expenditure in times of crisis works. It is a hard lesson we have learned after the 1929 economic crisis, which propagated for more than 10 years precisely because the idea that "the market would regulate itself" was still believed at the time. We have used this lesson after WWII, to rebuild a destroyed Continent. The US, and to some extent Europe, used it also after the 2008-09 crisis. And we are seeing it now once again, with COVID-19. All countries that are hit by the virus are planning to drastically increase their public expenditure. The absurdity here is that something that is very known and widely accepted by economists worldwide is portrayed as false at the most convenient time. It is simply illogical to expect that austerity measures would work in some circumstances and not in others. It has proven not to work with Greece, for example. The country, under the weight of new taxes and limited public spending, has lacked any growth for the good part of the last decade. As a result its debt has become more and more unsustainable. The IMF itself has recognized that austerity measures, often imposed in exchange of rescue packages, do not work.

4. Yes, one of the ways for a country to finance itself is via issuing debt. Debt, obviously, needs to be paid off with interests. Yet, countries are not the same as private citizens. They can also issue new currency (or "print money"). Issuing new currency creates inflation, which in turns helps diminishing the weight of public debt on a nation (as a loan that was taken 10 years ago is easier to repay after 10 years of inflation). To note, issuing currency is not the holy grail of macroeconomics: there are plenty of

examples of countries that did issue new currency just to run into hyperinflation and bankrupt. Venezuela is one of the most notable examples in recent times. However, here we are talking about Europe, the largest economic area in the world. The only way the ECB has issued new debt so far is Quantitative Easing. In simple words, the European Central Bank has bought billions of bonds, mostly government-issued. Most economists today agree that this is not an effective way to sustain growth. The US, for reference, is now thinking about giving directly money in the hands of consumers to tackle the COVID-19 crisis. Reality is that we are in uncharted waters when it comes to the real power of Central Banks and public debt. There are plenty of countries that failed in leveraging these powerful tools. But the European Union is large enough that it could try and experiment far more innovative and significant solutions.

Further, an important element that is conveniently not present in this narrative is how certain countries have benefited from a common currency. Companies operating in these countries (such as Germany or The Netherlands) have been made artificially more competitive by a euro that is weaker than their previous currency. In simple terms this means that even if they do not, for example, invest to renew their production machinery, they can still sell well because they are very cheap in the European market. On the other hand, companies in peripheral countries (such as Spain), have been made artificially less competitive by a strong euro. People that believe in the current structure of Europe will tell you that less competitive countries simply need to "become competitive" and follow the example of more virtuous nations. This is actually happening, but via lower salaries and decreased standard of living in certain European countries. What these people fail to mention is that the so-called virtuous nations have actually benefited from being *too* competitive.

Add to the above that Europe's geography puts specific countries at a deep disadvantage. Europe's "economic heart" stretches from London, Paris, The Netherlands, west and lower Germany, Switzerland and Northern Italy. Countries that are located further from these areas (for example Greece or Portugal) have a structural disadvantage versus the ones that operate there. Their goods have to travel longer to reach their clients and they have access to less capital at higher rates (given the absence of a banking union that would allow a Portuguese company to get a loan from, for example, a German bank).

In absence of a fiscal union and unable to compensate these factors with a depreciation of their own currency, public debt is *the* way that governments could compensate for these factors. Until the crisis of 2011-12.

In the previous paragraphs I tried to explain broadly why the mainstream narrative that is fed to European citizens is wrong. However, more worrying than the narrative itself is the fact this narrative has become the ONLY one in public debates. It has been used to polarize people and European citizens. If you do not agree with it, you must be one of those lazy Spaniards that wants money for free. If you agree with it, you have to agree with all of it. *Only if you do agree with all of it you truly are European*. Otherwise, you probably are uneducated or just in bad faith.

Why has this narrative taken place in Europe? Someone might argue that it is the hidden agenda of some European government to take over the Continent. While it is true that the current structure of Europe advantages some countries over others, it is my personal belief that this narrative has been pushed simply by inertia. It is a narrative that suits very well the status quo. In politics, the status quo is at a structural advantage. Up to the Treaty of Maastricht, European cooperation was mostly a matter of diplomacy and supranational cooperation that rarely involved public opinion. From the creation of the EU in 1992 in Maastricht, the European project has assumed a more concrete form for its citizens, with institutions legislating and even a common currency.

Yet, politics remained mostly at country level. As a result, politicians have had a far easier life in arguing for maintaining things as they were than for reforming them. Why, as a politician, should you waste energy in convincing your electors of unifying Europe? There is no gain for you and it will not impact your citizens' life in the short term. If anything there is a disincentive in arguing in favor of a new system where your current role would be resized and rendered less powerful. There is very little incentive for a politician to argue in favor of Europe, if not for some propaganda. It is easier, if anything, to argue against Europe. With time, it becomes a vicious circle. As there is no significant progress made with the Union, people perceive it at most as a powerless entity (which, in all fairness, it probably is in its current status), at worst as the cause of their problems. It then becomes even harder to argue in favor of it.

In the past 30 years, there has been no politician that was willing to push for the European project to complete. Single nation's agendas were always privileged. The simple narrative of "virtuous" and "lazy" countries was then born to support the easy option: nothing changes.

<u>**Why a United Europe?**</u>

In the previous chapters we have mentioned how a United Europe could actually benefit its citizens by reducing inequality, even if in the eyes of most voters this seems counter intuitive.

However, a reduction of inequality would not be the only benefit for a United Europe. A European Federal Budget to the tune of the USA (sized at 20% of GDP, versus the current 1%) would solve the issue of poor public budget management by specific countries. In plan terms, the less budget you give to Greece or Italy to spend, the better it is, based on history. Central governments are also far more difficult to infiltrate and to corrupt than local ones. By giving more budget to a central European authority, you are really killing two birds with one stone.

Of course, for this to make sense you have to make sure that the central authority that allocates the federal budget is reliable and *just*, following the principles of solidarity. The current structure of the European Parliament gives countries' representation based on their population. Countries like Germany, France and Italy get more seats in the parliament than Spain, Greece or Ireland. While this makes sense intuitively, it does not if it is to be applied to a redistribution rationale. If countries are represented according to their population, the federal budget will tend to be redistributed to those countries first. There would be a clear conflict of interest for a parliament that overwhelmingly represents 3-4 major countries to make decisions benefitting 27. It would need to be reformed, sooner or later. This is anyway the absurdity of the status of the European Union today: citizens in major countries such as Germany and France are unwilling to give more power to the European Parliament, even if they would be in the best position to benefit from it.

A fiscal union is a key point to achieve redistribution of wealth in Europe. But the benefits of a united Europe would not end there. A common market for services, for example, is something else that would benefit European citizens. Today, if you want to set up a company that provides any kind of service in all of Europe, you simply cannot. You have to still register with single countries' authorities. A banking union would also help citizens and companies in peripheral countries, giving them access to more funding opportunities and allowing them to tap into a larger market without bureaucratic issues.

Not to mention the benefits that would come from having a unified Europe in the international stage. Today the role of the EU in international matters is significant, especially in trade matters. However its weight is far below its potential. Heads of states still feel the need to negotiate and interact with single countries. There is no European bloc in this sense. We saw Donald Trump meeting with Angela Merkel and Emmanuel Macron, not with Jean Claude Juncker. A unified Europe with an elected president of some sort could change that.

<u>**COVID-19: the catalyst**</u>

People that do not want a United Europe will tell you that, at the end of the day, it is simply "not fair" to all live under one roof when we are so diverse. Why should I pay for those lazy Greeks with my tax money? This is a view that is deeply rooted in today's European society. It does not matter whether it is faulty and damaging for the future of Europe, it is there and it is difficult to eradicate.

I do not agree with this view, but I do not blame the people that share it. After all, today's standards of living in most of the EU are quite high. Surely they are not comparable to what they were after World War II. Is it really so bad for Greeks to put their public accounts in order? Is it really that bad if unemployment is a bit higher in Italy and Spain than in France or Germany? Is it even fair to compare forgiving war crimes with demanding that public money is spent wisely?

This brings me to the current COVID-19 situation. The debate on the current status of Europe will become meaningless, since the situation is about to get worse for everybody.

The effects of COVID-19 have been deep on the economies of all European countries. Nobody knows the real and final extent of the crisis, but there seems to be a certain agreement that things will not get back to normality until a vaccine is created and distributed in the population. This will have deep repercussions on the economies of Europe and far beyond.
For example, the psychological effects of a prolonged mass quarantine are unclear at this stage. The COVID-19 crisis is also putting immense pressure on existing European institutions. Countries that are hit the hardest, such as Spain or Italy, are requesting for financial and physical support at European level. The responses that they are getting so far are generally regarded as insufficient by the press. As of the moment of writing, no radical new measure or new institution has been introduced in Europe to face the COVID-19 crisis. All measures that have been proposed are coming from institutions that were already in place before the crisis. An example is the suggested use of the European Stability Mechanism by countries in need. This is an organization that

has in no way been thought to face a humanitarian crisis and substantially can just provide a line of credit to governments in need.

The COVID-19 crisis can be the catalyst that Europe needs to reform. The European Project slowly crumbled with inertia for the last 30 years. It fell victim of the relative wealth and economic strength that the European bloc enjoyed during this period of time. Its gradual collapse was fueled by local politicians instrumentalizing the EU and by an easy to understand, albeit false, mainstream economic narrative.

It is easier to "forgive and forget" the past when the present is in crumbles. Europe, all things given, was never in this situation since the 1950s. Possibly until now. The current humanitarian, economic and societal crisis determined by COVID-19 and by decades of stagnation can change Europe, if we play our cards right.

The manifesto

The European Union, today's take on the European Project, is perceived as a weak supranational institution. It is regarded as a technical, bureaucratic entity that is barely legitimated by some second-tier elections. Its most powerful institution, the European Parliament, is effectively a collection of second-tier politicians that are "sent to Europe" at the end of their careers. Its budget is just shy of 1% of Europe's GDP. After decades of stagnation and instrumentalization by local politicians, the European Union is far beyond recovery, in PR terms. So, let's start with a new name for the next chapter of a United Europe: the European Federation.

A European Federation should be built with a new world order in mind in order to tackle XXIst Century problems. 2020 European citizens need to feel that the advantages of a United Europe would widely compensate for its disadvantages.

In the short term, A new European Federation should be launched via two pillars:

1. A Green New Deal.

This would put Europe at the forefront of the great challenge of our century: making our contemporary economic system environmentally sustainable. In the last years, it has become more and more clear that the current economic system puts a significant strain on our environment. Europe should lead the world in investing in alternative mobility solutions, green energy, smart cities. The ultimate goal of a European green new deal should be to radically transform our society and make it sustainable via new technology, not by reducing standards of living. Specific examples of areas that a Green New Deal should tackle are:

- Invest in a pan european electric recharge road infrastructure. This would radically accelerate a 100% switch to electric vehicles. Today, charging points on main European roadways are scattered and unequally distributed between richer and poorer geographical areas. A new centrally thought infrastructure should ensure that any European citizen, no matter where resident, could buy an electric vehicle knowing that it could reach any major capital city in a few hours.

- o Invest heavily in R&D to improve battery technology and green energy sources. Today, it is simply not feasible for a major economic area like Europe to go 100% renewable. Green energy is simply not reliable enough, as it depends on winds, solar and other natural elements. The objective of this coordinated R&D investment should be to ensure that Europe can be powered at 100% by renewable energy. An immense technological challenge as of today technology, but one that can be solved within a few decades with the firepower of a United Europe.
- o Reinvent public transportation in all cities with more than 200,000 inhabitants. The objective should be to completely ban cars in these cities, once the public transport system is built to a 120-150% capacity based on the city's needs. To ensure smoothness and complete reliability, public transport even at local level should be directly financed by a central European budget.
- o Hyper-connecting major European hubs. New high speed train lines and hyperloops should connect all major European cities. The objective should be that any European citizen should never be more than 10 hours away from *any* major capital city in Europe. This will radically shorten distances and allow citizens to look for jobs and live in a geographically more vast area, improving mobility of labor.

This first pillar will boost European movement of people and will also benefit major industrial complexes in Europe, boosting employment in return. We are a Continent that is still based on relatively old industries, such as car manufacturing. This central boost to infrastructure will create thousands of jobs and increase the know-how of European firms, making them more competitive on the world's market as a result.

2. Universal basic income or universal basic services to all European citizens.

Job automation is a reality. Today, we could already virtually get rid of all truck or bus drivers in Europe. We do not, mostly because it would create a spike in unemployment and because our legal framework is not ready to get rid of a human element to blame if something goes wrong. This needs to change.

We should embrace machines and AI taking over jobs, not repelling it. It is the natural way we are intended to evolve as a species. If a machine is better at doing a job, then the job should be given to the machine. This is the only way to go if we are to eventually become a multi-planetary species.

Since the beginning of time we have been slaves of our labor as a species. As hunter-gatherers, we directly depended on our ability of hunting and gathering food. If we got sick, we could either hope to rely on our small community or die. As a sedentary species, things did not change for most of us. Few of us - usually kings and soldiers - could now afford to live off the labor of many others. Yet, as a species, we still needed to harvest fields and breed animals to survive. As our society evolved and got more and more sophisticated, this reality did not radically change. Today, we can either live off our labor (receiving a salary or selling something) or off our wealth (living with the money we accumulated or inherited). What changed is only *which* people could now live off the labor of others: we decided that nobility is not a thing and we gave this privilege to people that, in a way or another, earned it via their labor or inheritance.

The importance of labor is deeply embedded in us today. And for a good reason: it helped us evolve as a species. Religions flourished by putting the concept of labor at their center - protestantism, for example. Some countries still today base their Constitution on the right of having a job. In most of the world we are raised to believe that labor is holy, it is our way to find a sense of life. We are raised to believe that labor is - to some extent - even the sense of life itself. The "holiness" of labor has served well so far - it has effectively convinced most people to work hard to maintain a few.

However, as a species, not only we should move on but we *must* do it to evolve further. The power of human labor is limited to our physical and mental power. We got over our physical limits from the beginning of our sedentary life: using

animals to move. Using the flow of a river or a horse to power a mill. Then came the industrial revolution, the automobile, more powerful and sophisticated machines that helped us get over our physical limitations.
Today, we are slowly getting outmatched by machines in our mental power. There is no reason why we should resist. Only by letting this happen we can evolve and tackle more and more complex challenges as a human species.

Europe should be at the forefront of this change, once again experimenting it for the first time globally on a large scale. A Universal basic income is the only way to make this sustainable for our society. Ensuring that people will be provided for, even if their jobs are taken by more effective algorithms or machines. A European Universal Income should not be a charity to the poor. It should rather be the humble start of a Utopian society where everybody lives in comfort without the need - but with the option of - labor. These are the principles a European Basic Income should be based on:

- o It should be universal and free of other conditions. It should not be conceived as an unemployment benefit, but as a constant flow of money that citizens can rely upon for their entire life. It is in our nature to want more and to try and improve our condition. Citizens should therefore be free to have jobs on top of their basic income, to afford better and non-necessary things. A European Basic Income will actually encourage people in taking more risks, with either new jobs or entrepreneurial ventures. More entrepreneurs means more failures but also more successes. This will in turn improve our society from a macroeconomic perspective. We might finally witness the birth of European Tech giants and an actual European Silicon Valley.
- o It should be equally sized across Europe to make a decent living. Cost of living greatly varies within Europe. However, European Basic Income should be equally sized among countries. It should be sized to ensure a decent standard of living in the most expensive of European geographical areas. It should be just enough to cover rent, food and basic expenses in the suburbs of a large, generally expensive, European city. This, once again, will help movement of people. It will help repopulate marginal areas in the Continent.

People without high paying jobs or unemployed people will tend to migrate to cheaper cities. Together with a higher interconnectivity of Europe, it will help make Europe feel more united.

- It should be tied with inflation, at least. It should rise with inflation or, even better, with productivity of capital or labor. In the long run, an European Basic Income should guarantee a better and better standard of living, as algorithms and machines fully take over and render human input more and more redundant. In a future world where almost every citizen is rendered redundant, a basic income should not only cover their expenses but guarantee a great standard of living. Not having so would trigger social unrest.

Admittedly, a European Basic Income might not be feasible in this form from day one. Flooding European Citizens from one day to another with, for example, 2000 Euros per month, would probably trigger hyperinflation and create distortions in the economic systems. The first baby steps of a European Basic Income could come in the form of a European Unemployment Fund. But we should be quick to make this a stable and universal measure, ready for what's inevitable to come. As productivity of capital has risen in the last 30 years, productivity of labor has lagged behind and inequality has risen. This is a trend that is not going to stop: as jobs are substituted by algorithms, this will inevitably benefit the owners of capital. Shareholders of public companies and owners of private ones. On the other hand, as human labor is slowly rendered redundant, salary will decrease. This is a worrying trend that will trigger social unrest if it is not stopped. This is the great challenge that a European Basic Income should tackle.

It is not going to be easy to convince skeptics of basic income or idealists of labor. Some people believe that labor is noble, that it should be guaranteed. These people will go to great lengths to ensure that happens, even so far as to stop technological progress. They are no different than the people that in the past stuck to obsolete values and argued for stopping progress, even successfully at times. In the Ottoman Empire, the printing press was not adopted up until its final decades as it was thought to be incompatible with Islamic values. In middle-age China, less than wise Emperors decided to give up on world exploration as they preferred to focus internally. These people scored victories locally in the short term, but progress ultimately always won. The Ottoman Empire was ultimately rendered redundant and defeated by European nations. China lost its position as the world's economical and technological power.

Ultimately, there is always going to be someone who is open to progress and will render redundant those who are not. Europe today stands in front of a choice: adopting progress or be made redundant by someone else who will. In the short run, we can decide to ban autonomous vehicles, to impose human job quotas to private companies. These will be seen as victories and celebrated by people in the immediate term. In the long run, however, another country or economic bloc will get far ahead of us in economic and technological terms, rendering us redundant. What happens next is uncertain, but looking at history it will not look pretty.

If the above pillars are activated, there will surely be a new wave of pro-Europe thought across the continent. For those pillars to happen, Europe will need to reform not only its name but its institutions. This reform can happen at the same time or before the pillars. Below are some of the elements that, in my view, will need to change at some point in time:

- The European Parliament should be restructured so to represent each nation equally, no matter the population. National sentiment is too strong in Europe to think that a proportional system can work in the short term. Countries' representatives will do what's best for their citizens and it won't be fair to do so in a proportional system.
- A Fiscal Union should be imposed across European nations. Starting from a few selected taxes, fiscal income should be used to fuel Europe's central budget.
- A Federal budget of at least 20% of GDP should be constituted and given to the Parliament, in order for it to have actual firepower in all economic matters.
- A common market for services and banking union should be put in place.
- Europe should issue central debt as an only entity. At the same time local countries should also be allowed to issue debt on their own, as well as

regions and towns. This will privilege virtuous regions while keeping a mechanism of redistribution in place.

All of the above thoughts and recommendations are doomed to remain on paper, unless something starts to change for the better.

To change Europe, European citizens need to change first. This Manifesto is an open letter to any person that cares about the future of Europe. Act now, do your part!

<u>**2021 addendum**</u>

This book was first published in March 2020. The Paperback version comes in January 2021. Few months have passed, yet it seems a lifetime. During this time Europe announced a stimulus that pales in comparison to the USA.

The USA has already spent 2.2 Trillions USD in March 2020 and 0.9 Trillion USD in stimulus packages. Europe, in comparison, has planned a total stimulus of 0.75 Trillion EUR to be spent in 7 years. During the pandemic, European countries were not even able to coordinate between each other on what measures to adopt to curb the spread of the disease.

Sadly, these figures and facts talk for themselves for what concerns the future of the European Project.

About the Author

Roberto Bourboun is a passionate writer of contemporary politics and economics. Mother Tongue Italian and fluent in English. Self-published on Amazon Direct Publishing since 2020.

Stay in touch by visiting his Facebook Page at the address below:
 www.facebook.com/robertobourbonwriter.

This Paperback version has been launched exclusively on Amazon in 2021.